Joy
Overcomer
Unbreakable
Resilient
Newness
Evolving
Yoked

ONLY BY GOD'S GRACE

JODIAN HUTCHINSON

Acknowledgments

First and foremost, I want to thank the Author and Finisher of my faith, Jesus Christ. Without His chastening, reprimands, and as I like to say, "God draped me up," this book would not have been possible.

Secondly, I applaud myself for being obedient to the Holy Spirit. I never knew that writing a book was within me, but God revealed it. I would like to thank my sister-in-Christ, Tasshoya. When I jokingly said to her, "I feel like God is writing a book with my life," she simply replied, "Start writing." That moment pushed me forward.

Uncle Andrew, thank you for always believing in me. Dr Pastor Latoya Pinnock-Wilson, my children, Jenine and Bryan your constant support means more than you know.

Belinda, my editor, and Ekechi my graphic designer, I appreciate you both for being part of this journey and bringing it to manifestation. A book is like a fetus it needs care, nurturing, and love, and you both handled it with excellence.

To my parents, thank you for shaping the foundation of who I am today. God used every experience, even the difficult ones, to align me with His purpose. I honor and love you for your part in my story.

Auntie Colette, I am deeply grateful to you. When I shared the vision God gave me, you were steadfast. As an author yourself, you're always checking in, asking about my progress, and offering valuable insights. Your encouragement means the world to me.

To my communities of Queens, I appreciate every one of you. Your prayers and words of encouragement lifted me in ways I can't express.

Finally, to my doubters and naysayers, I appreciate you too. Romans 8:28 says, "And we know that all things work together for good to them that love God, to them who are the called according to His purpose." Without the challenges, how else would I have written this book? This book will be a blessing to many, and through it all, may God be glorified.

Contents

Introduction

My name is Jodian Hutchinson. I am a mother of two beautiful daughters and one wonderful son. I'm also a chef, running my own catering business. Today, I'm sharing my journey with you, as the Lord has led me to do. This book, "Journey," has been a long time coming. For a while now, I've felt the call to write it, but I kept delaying. We are all on a journey, whether we realize it or not. Along my path, I've asked myself these questions:

1. Where is my journey taking me?
2. Am I truly living, or merely surviving?
3. What lessons am I being taught?
4. Is my real purpose being fulfilled?

I encourage you to ask yourself these questions. Pray and ask God to reveal the answers.

This journey I'm about to share with you isn't just a collection of events—it's a testament to God's grace, His perfect timing, and His relentless pursuit of our hearts. My story, like many others, begins with a leap of faith, much like Abraham leaving his homeland. I had my own "Abraham moment" when I left Jamaica and found myself in Florida. I didn't have all the answers, but I had a word from God—just as Abraham did.

God doesn't always give us a detailed roadmap. Often, He calls us to step out in faith, to trust Him when it doesn't make sense, and to move even when we can't see the full picture. In my case, it wasn't just about relocating physically, but it was a spiritual journey too, one that involved letting go of comfort zones, past hurts, and self-doubt, to embrace His plan fully.

As I navigated the highs and lows of this path, God was molding me. There were moments of triumph when I felt like I was on the mountaintop, but there were also times when I found myself deep in the valley, questioning if I had made the right decision. And yet, in every valley, God was there, refining me, preparing me for greater things, just like He did with Elijah and Elisha.

This book is a contemplation of that journey—a mix of hills and valleys. It is about my personal walk with God, the lessons I've learned along the way, and the moments where His presence was undeniable, even amid my doubts. As you read, I pray you find encouragement for your own journey, knowing that no matter where you are—whether on the mountain or in the valley—God is with you, shaping you for something greater.

Chapter 1

My Abraham Moment

"Faith begins with a step."

Let's go on a journey, lol. My journey is long, but this is the part the Lord would have me share with you. Back in January 2021, I found out I was pregnant with what would have been my fourth child. I was excited—this is exactly what I wanted. I could barely provide for myself and the three I already had, but I was in love with the man of my dreams, and I wanted to give him a baby. How rude of me though, to not consult God about His plans for my life. The audacity, right? A whirlwind of events unfolded, and in March, I lost the baby. That moment was one of those times I would say, *"God draped me up"*. Another child wasn't part of His plan for me at that moment. I was devastated, furious even. I cried out to God, asking why He would allow me to get pregnant, only to take the baby away. It was through this loss that God showed me I wasn't the author of my own life—He was. He reminded me who was truly in control, His plans didn't align with the ones I had for myself. God wanted me to embark on a *Journey*, but I was so angry, I declined the offer, not realizing it was from Him. Then something shifted in my spirit. I remember saying, "Lord, be the pilot, and I'll be the passenger." That night, I fully surrendered every fiber of my being to God's will.

Just like Abraham, God brought me to a strange place, Florida. If you've read the story of Abraham, you'll understand what I mean. Read Genesis 12, and you'll see what God asked Abraham to do. In my case, I didn't realize I was living my own Abraham experience until later. This brings me to Jeremiah 29:11: "For I know the plans I have for you," declares the Lord, "plans to prosper you and not to harm you, plans to give you hope and a future." I came to Florida with basically an empty suitcase. People assumed I had planned not to return, but it wasn't my plan—it was God's. When I arrived, I was helping out with a family business and let me tell you, not every unfortunate situation comes from the devil. Like Job, sometimes God allows circumstances to unfold to bring out what He has already placed inside of us. He knows what needs to be done to push us toward His purpose.

Chapter 2
Out of My Element

"Faith move before it sees."

Let me be honest with you, I'm a Kingston girl, born and raised in Jamaica, so being in Florida was a real challenge for me. I'm more of a New York type of girl; I love the fast lane, the constant movement. Florida on the other hand, felt too confined, too slow for my liking. Yet this is where God needed me to be. It hasn't been easy. I've had plenty of *drape-ups* and bruises along the way, but I appreciate every one of them. Imagine a stubborn child, one you just told not to do something, or not to go around the corner, and what does she do? She goes anyway. That's me, Jodi, the hard-headed child. And instead of running to God crying when I fall, I dust myself off and take the lesson. That's why, when I encourage others, it comes from a place of true authenticity. I've been through it, and I wouldn't trade my relationship with the Lord for anything.

Chapter 3
The Test of Love and Faith

"You may encounter many defeats, but you must not be defeated."

- Maya Angelou

God knows us better than we know ourselves, and He knew I was hard-headed. He had to do something to keep me in place. So, here I was, finding myself in another relationship. Remember, I wasn't going back home, so I needed a way out. But before I go any further, let me say this: build a relationship with God first. Too many of us, me included, walk around with so much baggage. We put ourselves in unhealthy relationships, trying to fill voids that only God can truly fill.

Now back to that relationship. Oh boy, this one was a real eye-opener for me. This man opened his home to me for two years, and not once did he ask me to leave. It felt like divine provision, or so I thought. Was it truly God, or was I leaning on my own understanding? Or maybe I was so busy searching for love, I saw what I wanted to see. The way I behaved, there were times you would think the house was mine. He gave me a house, and in return, I gave him a home. You know, I have some good wife qualities (lol), but back to the story. We would have our altercations, and people would wonder why he never hit me. The presence of God surrounds me heavily, even to this day. My response was always, "God would have to give him consent to hit me."

Living with him, I fought so many spiritual battles. When I defeated the attacks in the spiritual realm, they would manifest in the physical. One moment stands out clearly. My best friend bought me a Pandora bracelet, and the night I received it, I had a vision about frogs. When I woke up the next morning and looked at myself in the mirror, I looked like a ghost. He saw me and asked why I looked so strange. My response was, "The Bible says the weapon will form, but it won't prosper." Later when we went out, I noticed my bracelet had turned black. I called my friend jokingly telling her we needed to get a refund because the bracelet had just changed color. She started explaining what she had learned about silver turning black, and it brought me back to that dream about the frogs. But even in the midst of that strange experience, I knew one thing—God was still in control.

Chapter 4
The Rollercoaster Ride of Love

" Your not stuck, you're being positioned."

Time went by, and I was still in the relationship, riding the highs and lows. Looking back, I can certainly laugh at myself. There were so many attempts to leave this man, but I just wouldn't do it. Let me tell you, black garbage bags don't have anything on me! Every time I decided I had enough, I would pack my bags, three or four garbage bags to be exact, while my bestie was on the phone, listening to me curse and rant. But the truth was, I wasn't going anywhere, lol. You think packing those garbage bags was hard? It was even harder when I had to ask myself where I would go, only to unpack and hang my clothes back up. What a toxic relationship, right? A beautiful girl like me, why did I think it was okay to settle? Do I regret my past relationships? No, because they only prepared me for the next great encounter. Just like in school, you can't move up a class without fulfilling what was taught in the previous one. Queens, when God is telling you to let go, trust that He has something better in store for you.

Chapter 5
The Turning Point

" Pulled back to be launched forward."

I found myself caught up in things I had no business being involved in. In 2022, God made it clear that I needed help; the spiritual attacks were wearing me down. It was time to commit my life to Him. I would wake up with bruises, looking like a ghost; attacked in my sleep, just to name a few. But through it all, God didn't leave me or forsake me. Our relationship was like anchor and sail; he wasn't a saint, and neither was I. He got into some illegal trouble, and I remember one particular drive to Miami that we thought was just a meeting at the FBI headquarters. That's what we were led to believe. When we arrived, I asked to use the restroom while he proceeded to his "meeting." On my way back to the car, I pushed the door open and saw federal agents surrounding the vehicle. If the ground could have opened up and swallowed me whole at that moment, I would have welcomed it. But once again, God came through. After he was locked up , I found myself stranded in Miami, unable to drive. My phone was buzzing with calls and messages from everyone who had heard what had happened. Panic set in as I realized I needed to get home. I scrambled to find a driver to help me retrieve the car, feeling the weight of the situation pressing down on me. In that moment, I understood the gravity of the circumstances and the chaos surrounding me. Yet even amidst the turmoil, I held on to the belief that God was still in control.

Chapter 6
Facing Consequences
and Learning Lessons

"There's purpose in the pain."

He's back home now, and we were figuring out which lawyer to hire for the case. Being around him taught me a lot. A couple of months later, God posed a question that shook me to my core: "Are you willing to pay the consequence?" With everything I was facing, the thought of me

going to prison was overwhelming. My father had served time, and I was determined to break that generational curse. I couldn't walk the same path. Sometimes in life, we take the wrong road and need to be redirected. I gained so much wisdom from God during this time. He showed me the importance of marriage and family, revealing the kind of relationship He desires from us. Take a moment to reflect on raising your child. No matter what they did, didn't you forgive them? How different is it with God? Or even marriage: when you had children, there were moments you craved quality time with your partner, away from the chaos of daily life. Let's be truthful with ourselves—God is seeking that same attention from us. He desires a close, intimate relationship, one where we prioritize Him above all else. Through this journey, I've learned that God's love and forgiveness are limitless, just as our love should be for those we care about. It's a humbling reminder that there's always a path back to Him no matter how far we stray.

Chapter 7
The Illusion of Divine Placement

"Transformed for testimony."

I found myself in a relationship I believed God had placed me in and I thought my life was finally coming together. Proverbs 3:5-6 reminds us to, "Trust in the Lord with all thine heart; and lean not unto thine own understanding. In all thy ways acknowledge Him, and He shall direct thy paths." I was leaning on my understanding and holding on to an unhealthy relationship. No matter the chaos, I wouldn't let go of this relationship. In my heart, I was planning my baptism and wedding back-to-back, convinced that everything would work out. Sometimes we set our hearts up for heartbreak and then argue with God about it. I had everything for my wedding planned out, yet I knew deep down that this man couldn't truly help me. Nevertheless, I clung to the hope that I would get married. I had faith that God would throw the case into the sea of forgetfulness. How many times would Jodi find the man of her dreams only to get draped up right? How gullible was I to think that my desires were aligned with God's plans for me? In spite of all I thought and did, God never left me; He is faithful.

Three days before I was set to say, "I do," God intervened. I cried, and it was in that moment I truly learned the meaning of Isaiah 55:8-9, "For my thoughts are not your thoughts, neither are your ways my ways, saith the Lord. For as the heavens are higher than the earth, so are my ways higher than your ways, and my thoughts than your thoughts." God's plan always supersedes our own. This led me to ask myself: Are you fully surrendering your plans to God? It reminded me of a child who disobeys her parents by going shopping, when she was told not to, only to return every item. That was me—returning everything I had bought for our wedding that God didn't say "yes" to. Once again, I found myself getting draped up, but this time, it was for a purpose.

Chapter 8
Restoration and Revelation

"Delay isn't denial-it's alignment."

I *did* get baptized, just not married. Life continued, and I found myself packing my garbage bags every now and then. If God doesn't want you somewhere, trust me, you can never be truly happy. I know this all too well. We started a food trailer business that received remarkable reviews. I had a passion for food in high school, but somewhere along the way, I lost it. This venture reminded me of Joel 2:25-26, "And I will restore to you the years that the locust hath eaten, the cankerworm, and the caterpillar, and the palmerworm, my great army which I sent among you." God never fails. Every weekend, people were looking for our scrumptious jerk meals, not to mention our seventeen jerk sauces. Business was booming. Months passed, and my ex gave his life to God, a transformation I had been praying for. As a child of God, it's a deep desire to see your partner walking alongside you, so I was very excited for him. But soon after, I found myself questioning God about marriage again. Everything looked good in my eyes now. We were both baptized, so why couldn't we get married? I was in a storm that was shaping me, but all I could see were problems. I started to do what any good woman would do; I fasted and prayed on his behalf, still convinced he was my husband. I prayed fervently that he wouldn't have to serve time. One morning, the Holy Spirit gave my mother a word to share with him. She said, "God said you have to do some time. You have done so much already and gotten away, but not this time." That revelation shifted my perspective. Deep down, I was still holding on to faith in God, trusting that He knew what was best for both of us.

The Catapult Experience

I want to share with you a story from the Bible—the story of the woman with the issue of blood. Her faith in Jesus led to a catapult experience, a moment that changed everything for her. A catapult is like a slingshot; if you don't pull back with force, it will never reach its target. This woman suffered for twelve long years, and finally, God decided it was time for the stone to be launched forward. You might wonder how it was possible for this woman to endure such a condition for so long. She sought help from many physicians, but none could assist her. That struggle was like pressure building up behind the slingshot. Think about her situation; she likely had a family. Imagine being away from your husband and kids, labeled as unclean. This added even more force behind the slingshot. But then she heard about Jesus and the miracles He performed. (Matthew 9:20-21) "And behold, a woman, which was diseased with an issue of blood twelve years, came behind Him, touched the hem of His garment: For she said within herself, if I may but touch His garment, I shall be whole." At that moment, the slingshot was catapulted. All that pressure she had endured transformed into faith being lifted. The more pressure you undergo, the higher your faith can rise. When you experience a catapult moment, your worries fade away, God cleans your slate. When something is catapulted, it doesn't travel along the ground and risk being delayed; it soars through the air. The woman with the issue of blood wasn't the only one who experienced this catapult moment that day; Jairus's daughter had her own miraculous experience too.

Side note: Change your posture; God can catapult you anytime He chooses. So don't grow weary.

(1) What is it that you want God to catapult you into at this moment?

(2) How is your faith?

(3) Are you giving up on the journey?

Chapter 9
Reassurance

"Purpose won't let you quit."

Time went by, and I grew closer to God, still taking the hits that life threw at me. Being away from my kids and only being able to speak with them via video calls was definitely a challenge. I remember calling my mom on my eldest daughter's birthday, crying my eyes out. They just laughed at me—oh my, lol. I was so attached to my kids, and being so far away really took a toll on me. When my youngest daughter graduated from primary school, I wasn't there, yet God gave me my own encounter during that time. God speaks to us every day, but the question is, are you listening? On the day of my daughter's graduation, God was speaking to me, and I simply followed the leading of the Holy Spirit. The topic He gave me that day was "Well." I started doing my research online, and then I heard God say, "Go deeper." So I did, and let me share what God revealed to me. In Genesis 26:20-24, Isaac was digging a well, but the herdsmen of Gerar stopped him. God revealed to me that He caused the herdsmen to derail Isaac because He needed Isaac to find the right well. Sometimes, we need to get thrown off course to be rerouted to where God needs us to be. Isaac kept digging and eventually found the right well, which he called 'Rehoboth.' He then proclaimed a word over his family and herdsmen. That same night, God appeared to Isaac and assured him that it was done; the word He proclaimed was signed and sealed. That morning, the Holy Spirit nudged me to post about my youngest daughter and speak a word over her life. It didn't make sense to me at the time, but I eventually gave in. Sometimes, when you get that feeling, that's the Holy Spirit, trust it. After reading Isaac's story, God gave me Jeremiah 29:11 to speak over my children. A few hours later, it was time for the graduation ceremony to begin. I received the pamphlet, and there was my daughter's name, right next to Jeremiah 29:11. I cried so hard and said, "God, You gave me my own Isaac moment." The Bible says that when Isaac proclaimed the word, the Spirit of the Lord visited him that same night. God used the word He gave me for my daughter to speak over the entire graduating class. God is so faithful. That moment confirmed what God had been telling me all along—my children are covered under His wings. Habakkuk 2:3 tells us to write the vision and make it plain, and that's exactly what I did. To this day, whenever I start to worry about my kids, the Holy Spirit reminds me of Jeremiah 29:11, and it calms me down.

Chapter 10
Isolation Time

"You're graced for this."

My ex was in and out of court, and I was praying that the case would get thrown out. Listen, you couldn't find anyone more committed to God than I was at that time. I was on prayer lines, attending fasting services. No matter the time, I was there. After all, I thought he was my husband. They put an ankle monitor on him, and he had to be home by 12 a.m. and he couldn't leave before 8 a.m. His hustling was on pause, and he had to return to a 9-5. Yours truly was at home, playing wife, cleaning the house, and having hot meals ready by the time he got home. Even then, I was still packing my garbage bags when we argued.

To any young girl reading this, love yourself first. Find your true, authentic self, the version God created you to be. These streets aren't playing.

Time was winding down for his sentencing, and who do you think couldn't stop crying? Yep, that was me. The day came, and the judge made his decision. The crime was serious enough to warrant

10 years, but God remained faithful. What was supposed to be 36 months got reduced to 24, and then finally to 18 months. I still believe that was God. He was sentenced, but he was still walking around Florida. People found that strange, but I said it was all God. October came, and it was time for him to turn himself in. God was all over this situation. They even allowed him to drive himself to the facility where he was supposed to serve his time. Friday arrived, and it was time to say goodbye. I tried my best not to break down, but I did. The Lord told me to pray for him, and I ended up doing just that.

We usually went out on Fridays to sell food, but now I had to do it by myself. I stood in the living room, crying my eyes out, saying, "God, it's just us now. I know You did this to get my full attention—I'm all Yours." You can't just surrender once; surrendering and repentance should be done daily. Evening came, and it was time to go sell the food. How could I do this on my own? I was so used to my ex being there. I broke down again, crying uncontrollably. How could he leave me to handle this all alone? But then, in the midst of it all, I heard a small voice. It was my nephew JJ's voice saying, "Come on, Auntie Jodi, you got this." It was something he would have actually said. I washed my face, called my driver, and went out to sell the food I had prepared.

Identifying My Struggles

Here I was, being isolated once more—*drape up* again. God started stripping me down, showing me my faults, my weaknesses. Isolation, though hard, turned out to be the best thing that ever happened to me. I couldn't hear God properly before, because my ex had become my idol.

What or Who Is Your Idol?

Sometimes we idolize things or people without even realizing it. I was so busy trying to prove my worth to a man who couldn't even see it. But here's the truth: God never gave him the clearance to see my value. I was the right package, but I was at the wrong doorstep. I remember God asking me, "If you know your value, why are you busy proving it to someone else?" That question made me check myself. I know a lot of people can relate to this. We're so starved for love that we will accept anything that looks or even smells like it. But then, the scales began to fall from my eyes. My healing journey had finally begun.

Have You Started Your Healing Process?

Healing or *Refuah*, which is from the root word *Rapha*, means to repair, restore, or make healthful.

You might wonder why I'm using the Hebrew meaning. Well, Hebrew and Greek definitions give a deeper understanding of what God is saying. I started to see things the way God wanted me to, but I was still in disbelief. I remember singing a song, and I was intentional with it, asking God to show me Jodi through His eyes. When you're intentional in your worship and prayer, the atmosphere shifts. I began to see myself in ways I had never seen before. Even my conversations with my ex were totally different. I was learning what discernment was, as God opened my spiritual eyes. I even went to Him and asked, "Are you sure this person I'm now seeing and hearing is really me?" I gained wisdom and knowledge that I hadn't had previously, but I was still focused on the pain. I remember saying, "God, how could you bring me to a strange place, take me away from my kids? And not only that, but take away the person who was my support system?"

Chapter 11
Purpose cannot Die

"You are choosen and equipped."

G od started pruning me into who He called me to be, not who I thought I was.

Jeremiah 1:5 says, "Before I formed thee in the belly I knew thee; and before thou camest forth out of the womb I sanctified thee, and I ordained thee a prophet unto the nations." I remember saying, "God, explain." He responded, "Look at the Israelites. I didn't create them to become slaves, but they adopted the slave mentality and believed it." We are all prisoners of our thoughts until we let God in so He can release us. We give our minds too much control over our lives. The mind is where thoughts get processed, and we often give it far too much power. We must learn to put our thoughts under subjection and in alignment with the Word of God. The Bible reminds us we don't wrestle against flesh and blood, but against principalities and rulers in high places. Our thoughts are spiritual, whether good or bad. Positive thoughts lift you up; negative thoughts keep you buried. So I ask, what are you doing to change that trajectory?

I got sick, but I'd call it a spiritual attack. Each time I finished my medication, I found myself back at the doctor's office. After my third round of medication, I reached my breaking point. That Sunday, I cried out to God, and I was instantly healed.

With the business on pause for the festive season, when things naturally slow down, I asked God for direction. I wanted my next step to be fully in His will.

Soon, an opportunity opened for me to work as a line cook at a downtown Fort Lauderdale hotel restaurant. Now listen, Jodi didn't have any qualifications for a place like that! All I'd known was running my little food trailer. Yet, in that moment, I saw Proverbs 18:16 come alive: "A man's gift maketh room for him, and bringeth him before great men." God's hand was undeniably at work. No certificates, no fancy experience, *only God* could have made that happen. On my first day, I didn't even have my own knife to work with. I had zero experience in a kitchen of that caliber, but I walked in, ready to see where He would take me. And during all of this, I continued to hang onto that relationship. I guess part of me still wanted to be the "good woman." Jamaicans would say, "She a yamhead"—stubbornly staying even when it's clear there's nothing there to hold onto. Why did I need the world's validation? God was clearly pulling me away, and yet, I kept clinging, trying to get fire from a heap of wet coals. I hadn't stopped to ask God what His plans were for the relationship. This was a season of wrestling, *between my will and His plan.*

Chapter 12

Stepping in the Unknown

"Small steps birth big shifts."

It was February 2022 when I had a dream of my friend saying, "The Holy Ghost said, you must move." I woke up confused and started questioning God; *He was silent*. Just imagine, no answer, only silence from God. I spent weeks crying, asking, "How am I supposed to move if this is the man I'm meant to marry?" But there was no response.

Instead of answers, God started revealing areas in me that needed fixing. Lesson learned: always be willing to search yourself. Through this quiet season, He showed me my brokenness. I realized I'd been craving love so much that I kept putting myself in unhealthy relationships. I knew it was time for change, but change couldn't happen until I was intentional about my relationship with God.

I began asking God to search me, to show me my flaws. I remember sharing my thoughts with my mom, hoping for her understanding, but her response wasn't what I expected. Frustrated, I went back to God and asked what was wrong. He told me, "You are seeking love from your mother, but she can't give you what she didn't receive." That truth hit me hard. I spent the next hour just walking and talking with God. It was time for a serious decluttering of my life.

The time had come for me to step into who God called me to be, *not* who society told me I should be. I was so broken, exhausted from chasing validation that was never mine to seek. The Hebrew word for broken is *Shabar*, which means crushed, exhausted, depressed, oppressed, shattered. That was me, Shabar in every sense—emotionally, mentally, and spiritually. But God had His own plan for healing each part of me.

Chapter 13
Embracing Healing

"Beauty rises from brokenness."

H ere I was, completely open to God, asking Him to enter my heart and remove everything standing in His way. I had to revisit painful conversations and moments from my past, especially those with my mother about her upbringing. It was hard, and I wanted to run from all the hurt and pain. But healing often waits for us in those uncomfortable places we avoid. We are no longer the broken children we once were; we have the power to overcome what tries to keep us captive. In John 16:33, Jesus tells us He has overcome the world. When God reveals something to us, it's not to hurt us but to help us find the root cause and truly heal. If we don't destroy the root, the pain will keep resurfacing. I realized my mom couldn't show me the love I craved because she never received it herself. That lack of love made my childhood difficult. I grew up yearning for affection, and as an adult, I ran to what I thought was love, only to add more brokenness to the pieces already there. I was lacking self-love. Have you taken the time to love on yourself? For many of us, it's a challenge to even look in the mirror and speak life into the person staring back.

But developing this habit is crucial. Speak God's promises over yourself: "I am fearfully and wonderfully made" (Psalm 139:14), "I can do all things through Christ who strengthens me" (Phil 4:13), and "Greater is He that is in me than he that is in the world" (1 John 4:4). When I look in the mirror, even amidst the storms, I remind myself, "No, Queen, after all you've been through, you still look this good." I thank God for His grace and mercy. His love makes us glow from within, and a heart full of gratitude will start to flourish.

True Healing Through Forgiveness

God spoke to my heart, saying, "You're busy seeking love from everyone else when I love you effortlessly." He reminded me of His promise in Psalm 27:10: "When my father and my mother forsake me, then the Lord will take me up." God's promises are true and steadfast. Yet, dealing with brokenness comes with layers of healing that require us to face the parts of ourselves we often suppress. God told me it was time to truly forgive my mother. I argued back, "God, I have forgiven her." But He gently revealed, "If you speak of hurt and don't feel peace, there is still a stronghold over you." We often suppress pain subconsciously, but God wants us to invite Him in and confront it head-on. Only then can true healing and freedom begin.

The Depth of Forgiveness

In Hebrew, forgiveness is *Naga*, meaning pardon, leniency, and mercy. God, in His wisdom, allowed a situation to happen that revealed I had not fully forgiven my mother. When she spoke to me, it triggered a part of my childhood, and I found myself reacting not as the older, more mature version of me but as the little girl still carrying that pain. This was a spiritual eye-opener, and though I hadn't visited a therapist, God Himself became my counselor. Forgiveness, I learned, is not something we can declare lightly. God illustrated this by letting me witness something unusual: a cockroach egg hatching. The baby roaches, or nymphs, emerged white, not the familiar brown of adult roaches. This visual lesson struck me deeply. God began to teach me about unforgiveness. He explained, "Just as those nymphs are initially white, unforgiveness often appears hidden or subtle, but it multiplies and transforms over time."

Unforgiveness breeds bitterness, anger, envy, hatred, and even sickness. God also revealed that some aspects of unforgiveness are deceptive. We may think we have forgiven, but deeper inspection can reveal branches of resentment we never recognized. Like understanding the true nature of the roach nymphs, we need God to expose hidden strongholds. I entered a season of deep prayer and fasting, even refraining from communication with my mother during this time. It was a season of spiritual cleansing, not something to be rushed or taken lightly. Dealing with unforgiveness is like ridding a house of an infestation. You can't simply declare the house clean; you need pest control to locate and destroy the nest. Similarly, true forgiveness requires us to dig deep, confront our pain, and let God bring full restoration.

The Weight of Unforgiveness

The process of truly forgiving is no quick journey; it's a journey of unearthing wounds that we may not even know we've buried. I discovered that God wasn't finished with my childhood; He wanted to address things I had long suppressed, things I thought were hidden away for good. When we surrender to God, we can't give Him just part of our hearts; He requires it all.

Surrendering means allowing Him to cleanse every part of us, leaving no residue for the enemy to exploit.

It wasn't easy to confront the things I'd kept silent about, even with myself. But God told me it was time to let go, and that meant facing memories I hadn't spoken of. I had to call my mom and tell her I remembered a painful incident—and that I forgave her. I reached out to my aunt as well, even though she acted as if she didn't remember what I was talking about. And that was okay; I was on a mission to free my younger self. Not everyone will understand or acknowledge your apology, but that shouldn't stop you. This process wasn't about anyone else's response; it was about releasing my own soul. With each act of forgiveness, I felt lighter, as if I was being renewed. With God's work in me was just beginning; He *draped me up* again to reveal even more. The subconscious can store an incredible amount of pain, and God began to show me just how many people and memories I still needed to release. It was overwhelming—so much hurt wrapped up in one person. I realized that carrying all that bitterness and anger wasn't hurting anyone but myself. Unforgiveness is a heavy, ugly thing, piling up layer upon layer of resentment, rage, and bitterness. And the more I released, the more I was able to experience a peace I hadn't known. I began to understand that true freedom lies in letting go, not only of past pain but also of the control I thought I had over my own healing.

Releasing the Prisoners

One evening after a long day at work, I found myself reflecting on a conversation I had with a friend about forgiveness. She had been open about her own journey and shared a song with me: "Heal My Heart" by Jermaine Edwards. When I finally listened to it, something cracked wide open within me. The lyrics seemed to touch wounds I didn't even realize I still carried. Tears flowed freely and uncontrollably, and in that moment, I knew God was revealing deeper layers of my heart that needed healing. I had buried so many people in the prison of my subconscious, including my children's father and my own father. The Holy Spirit led me to write an apology letter to my children's father, releasing him from the resentment I had held onto for so long. I don't think he ever fully understood the depth of what happened that day when he received the message. But it wasn't about him; it was about setting myself free.

Then it was time to face my feelings toward my father. I had convinced myself that there was no hurt there, that we were good because he had supported me financially. But as God peeled back the layers, I saw the truth: I resented him for his absence, for not being there to guide me, love me, and teach me the things a father should. Financial support had never been enough to fill that void. God's revelation was a painful one, but it was necessary.

Parents, this is a clarion call for you: don't get so consumed by the role of provider that you forget to be present in your children's lives. Society may push the importance of material support, but children need more than that—they need love, guidance, and quality time. The void left by an absent parent doesn't heal on its own. Forgiveness can be a path to healing, but it's much better when you're truly there for your children from the beginning. This journey taught me the importance of constantly seeking the hidden places in my heart, places where unforgiveness might still lurk. Releasing these "prisoners" wasn't just about freeing them; it was about freeing myself to live fully in the purpose God had for me. As I forgave and let go, I could feel myself becoming lighter, closer to who He created me to be.

Chapter 14
Spiritual Cleansing

"The cleanse makes room for the call."

E ven though I was still in the relationship, I knew God was calling me to something higher. I stayed in that apartment, paying bills and hoping God would change His mind about my ex. But God began to open my spiritual ears, allowing me to hear conversations that revealed things I couldn't ignore. The spiritual warfare within those walls was intense, but I was determined to fight.

One evening, after work, the Holy Spirit nudged me: "Go home and pray through the house." I agreed, though by the time I got home, I was exhausted. I took a shower, hoping to settle in, but the prompting persisted—get the olive oil and pray out the house. Finally, I obeyed. As I sat on the bed praying, something remarkable happened; my spiritual eyes opened. I could see beyond the physical realm, and I was shocked at what was revealed. There on my dresser were two ceramic pieces, decorative heads I thought nothing of. But the Holy Spirit showed me that these were Buddha heads. I hadn't even realized it when I bought them, thinking they were just decorative items to beautify my home. But now, God was showing me that they were open doors for spiritual oppression. I started to pray, questioning, "Lord, are You sure?" And yet the images were clear—a man and a woman, spirits I hadn't invited but had unknowingly welcomed.

When I finished praying, I looked up Buddha images online, and there it was, a clear resemblance. I realized why I'd often felt watched, why I'd been pleading with God to mute any monitoring spirits. I had allowed the enemy into my home through what I thought were harmless decorations. I had two by my bedside and two on the dresser, facing my bed.

It was a hard lesson. I realized how easily the enemy could use what we love to set up strongholds. I scooped those heads up and placed them in the garbage room. At first, I left them in the garbage room, but the Lord gently corrected me: "Why would you want to release those spirits into someone else's home?" I understood the message, so I took them to the chute and threw them away for good. In that moment, I learned that spiritual discernment and obedience are not just about what we believe but about how we guard our lives and homes. Our eyes may see one thing, but in the spiritual realm, everything has weight and consequence.

Chapter 15
The Mother and Father Blessing

"Blessed by their prayers, built by His grace."

My journey to Atlanta unfolded in a way that showcased God's orchestrating hand. Initially desiring to attend a marriage retreat, I lacked the funds but trusted in God's will. Eventually, an opportunity arose for me to be the chef for the event, aligning with God's timing for me to move into a new season. Amid obstacles and uncertainties, I persevered, reaching Atlanta for the retreat. To my surprise, I discovered a couple with the same last name, Hutchinson, serving as the main speakers. As the retreat progressed, God orchestrated a divine encounter where the pastor and his wife spoke blessings into my life. Standing in front of strangers, the pastor and his wife, with the same last name, delivered father and mother blessings. This unexpected moment revealed God's intricate plan, providing me with the blessings I had sought from my parents. It was a powerful reminder that God's ways are beyond our understanding, and the journey of forgiveness is a continuous process, culminating in unexpected and beautiful outcomes. My experience mirrored the biblical narrative of Elisha proceeding despite obstacles, ultimately reaching a destination filled with divine blessings. It underscored the truth that God completes the process, and His timing and plans surpass human comprehension. The journey toward forgiveness is a dynamic and transformative process, revealing God's faithfulness and grace.

So there I was back from Atlanta, thinking once again that I'm fully healed of unforgiveness. But let me tell you, be prepared to close every door that unforgiveness has opened in your life. I had so much baggage, carrying around childhood trauma, lack of love, rejection, self-sabotage, and a deep need for attention, just to name a few. But God, in His faithfulness, was diligent in exposing each and every one of them. It wasn't an easy process. Every time I thought I was done, God revealed another layer, another door that needed to be closed. I realized that healing isn't a one-time event. It's a continuous journey, an ongoing process. Each step brought me closer to becoming the person God intended me to be. As God exposed the broken areas in my life, He didn't just leave me there. He provided the tools and the strength to work through them. Each time I surrendered another piece of myself, He replaced it with His love and His truth: the truth that I am fearfully and wonderfully made. The truth that I am loved, not for what I do or who I am in the eyes of others, but simply because I am His. It's not easy to face the things we have buried deep inside. But I realized that those things will continue to affect us, even in ways we're not aware of, until we allow God to bring them to the surface and heal them. For so long, I had been walking around with a smile on my face, trying to be strong for everyone else, while inside, I was broken. I was carrying the weight of my past, and it was affecting every part of my life—my relationships, my self-worth, even my ability to fully trust God. But God is patient. He never rushed me through the process. Instead, He walked with me, step by step, showing me the areas that needed to be healed and giving me the strength to face them. He taught me that true healing doesn't come from ignoring the pain or pretending it doesn't exist. It comes from facing it head-on, acknowledging it, and then allowing God to heal it. Through this process, I've learned to forgive—not just others, but also myself. I've learned that forgiveness is a gift you give yourself. It's releasing the hold that the past has on you and stepping into the freedom that God has for you, and that freedom is beautiful. So here I am, still on this journey of healing, still learning, still growing. I know I am not alone; God is with me, guiding me, and I trust that He will complete the good work He has started in me.

Chapter 16
Still a Work in Progress

"Healed people heal others."

I can only speak about my journey. The more God healed me, the more I availed myself to Him to work on me. When God finally brought me out of the pit of unforgiveness, it was time for us to conquer the next demon. By this time, I could identify unforgiveness and had no intention of returning to that pit. At night, after work, God and I would have our conversations. I remember one particular conversation: "God, I want a husband who will love me like Jesus loves the church. But, not my will be done, only Thy will be done." Less than a week later, a man appeared. We began courting, and this man matched who God called me to be—not who I was before. Please read that line again. To be honest, this courtship took a whole different trajectory. This man is caring, loving, God-fearing, family-oriented, and principled, just to name a few qualities. It was hard for me to accept the love God was using him to pour into me. Do you remember what I prayed and asked God for? When you pray, ask God for the capacity to maintain that which you prayed for. On days when I couldn't love myself, this man would be there to pour love into me. I would receive random messages saying, "I'm proud of you" or "I love you." I became convinced something had to be wrong with this man—who says and sends so much love like that? But the truth was, something was wrong with someone, and it wasn't him—it was definitely Jodi.

I started to put on my running shoes, because naturally, the easiest thing to do is to run away from what you don't understand, right? But God told me to relax and breathe. This is where Bryan came in and began teaching me about what I was feeling and how to express those feelings. In that moment, Jodi learned that it wasn't about running—it was about understanding her emotions and how to deal with them.

Here I was, at a broken place, thinking I knew what love was; but God said, "Let me show you what love truly is." Every time I stepped onto the battlefield, it was rough. At 38 years old, I thought I had life figured out, yet I didn't even have an ounce of the life I should've been living. I have to give God thanks for His refining fire. When He's finished refining you, you won't even recognize yourself. As Job 23:10 says, "But He knoweth the way that I take: when He hath tried me, I shall come forth as gold."

A simple *yes* to God and put your warrior suit on, because the battlefield is no playground. The process of transformation is much like that of a caterpillar waiting to become a butterfly, or grapes being pressed to become fine wine, or a kimberlite turning into a diamond. It's all a process, but the real question is: Are you willing to submit to God's process?

Chapter 17

Love through the valley

"God timing is never late."

There were so many times I wanted to run away from this partnership. But let me tell you this: God always uses someone to be a blessing to us. Remember that. Here I am at 38, experiencing feelings I didn't understand. Pain creates so much void in your life, and you may think you're living your best life, but it's just an illusion. I charge you to pray and ask God what needs to be uprooted, what needs to be healed. I had to look in the mirror and tell the younger version of myself that it was okay to let go, and that the older version of me would survive. It became a regular routine. Most of us can't do the mirror talk—it took me a while to truly look myself in the eye and have that conversation with my younger self. Sometimes, all that part of you needs to hear is, "I love you. I'm sorry for all we went through, but I'll take care of the person I am now."

Serving God means there can't be anything hidden. If you are truly honest with Him, God will clean every corner of your life—

every single one. That molestation they said you lied about, the abortion, the expectations you placed on your parents, give it all to God and watch Him give you beauty for ashes. He's still in the restoration business. As His word says in Joel 2:25: "And I will restore to you the years that the locust hath eaten, the cankerworm, and the caterpillar, and the palmerworm, my great army which I sent among you."

God used Bryan to teach me about the emotions I was experiencing. I learned to feel, to acknowledge them, to process them, but if they didn't line up with God's will, I didn't let them take root. I was so used to being this independent woman. I had never had a man cater to my needs until now, and I never knew how to truly be a woman until now. I took the disrespect, neglect, cheating—all that—and thought it was love. Who was I fooling, thinking if I stayed in those unhealthy relationships, those men would change?

Being totally transparent, I never knew someone like Bryan existed. You know those thoughts that tell you there's something better than what you're experiencing right now? Well, there is! And those thoughts were God giving you hope deep inside. Let me tell you, I pinched myself for about a month because I was convinced I was dreaming. Up until now, I'm still amazed. But guess what? There are so many promises in the Word of God that we can hold on to. Like Jeremiah 29:11, "For I know the thoughts that I think toward you, saith the Lord, thoughts of peace, and not of evil, to give you an expected end." Or Psalm 84:11, "For the

Lord God is a sun and shield: the Lord will give grace and glory: no good thing will He withhold from them that walk uprightly."

God's word never lies. Trust the process. Psalm 23:4 shows how David trusted his process. What I love about that verse is that David didn't run or ride a donkey; he walked through the valley, enduring every bit of the process. It hasn't been easy for me either. Matthew 16:24 says, "Then Jesus told His disciples, 'If anyone would come after me, let him deny himself and take up his cross and follow me.' " You have to lose habits, people, and anything that's not aligned with God.

Chapter 18
Dying to Self

"Crucified flesh, resurrected faith."

I started to deny myself, finally accepting the love being poured out on me. The Lord began to show me the things that needed to go: the secret clout chasing, pride, low self-esteem, people-pleasing—just to name a few. I had just moved into a rented room and loved my new space. I was excited.

I was working in a new space, with Bryan in the picture, and you could say I was walking in answered prayer. As I settled into my new space, I began to realize just how much God was stripping away from my life. The secret clout chasing, the pride, the need for validation from others—all of it was starting to fall off. It didn't happen all at once, but the more I stayed in God's word, the more I saw the things that no longer belonged. It wasn't easy, but consistency and dedication to God's process made it possible.

In this new season, Bryan remained a significant part of my life. Here I was, in a space that I had prayed for, working a job, and experiencing the love I had asked God for. Everything seemed to be coming together, but I learned quickly that new blessings come with new battles. There's always warfare before a breakthrough. The storm may come, but after every storm, there's a calm. And in that calm, I could sense God was doing something new in me. Even in the midst of answered prayers, I knew there was more work to be done. You see, many of us are quick to blame others for our downfall. It's easier to play the blame game than to face ourselves. But as God began to do a deeper work in me, I realized something important: when you point one finger at someone else, there are four pointing back at you. None of us are perfect. We all have inner work that needs to be done. And so I had to ask myself, who am I letting do that work? Am I letting the world shape me, or am I letting God refine me? That's when the real transformation started. Letting God do His work within me required a surrender I wasn't always ready for, but it was necessary. God was molding me, shaping me, teaching me how to truly walk in His will, not in the opinions of others or in my own brokenness. As I continued to walk this journey, I learned that God's work is often uncomfortable, but it's always for our good.

Chapter 19
Humble Servant

"Obedience is the language of a servant."

After all the inner work that God was doing in me, there was another big shift coming. It was time to face my calling. I knew deep down that God had been preparing me for something bigger than myself, but stepping into it felt intimidating. I had seen glimpses of it through my catering business and how I'd touched people's lives with food, but there was more. God had planted dreams in me that I hadn't fully embraced yet. One of the biggest challenges of stepping into my calling was battling my own doubts. You see, even though I had been through so much healing, there was still this voice in the back of my mind that whispered, "Who do you think you are?" It was the enemy trying to sow seeds of insecurity and fear. But this time, I was better equipped. I had learned to recognize those voices for what they were—distractions meant to keep me from fulfilling God's purpose in my life.

Around this time, my business, Nerdermar Catering, was also going through changes. God was showing me how to use it not just as a service but as a ministry. I began to realize that feeding people wasn't just about the food. It was about serving them with love and care, pouring into their spirits through every interaction. This shift in perspective helped me see that my business was also part of the calling that God had for me. There were moments where I questioned if I was ready for it all. The vision felt too big, but I reminded myself that God doesn't call the qualified—He qualifies the called. So I stopped trying to have all the answers and started trusting God to guide each step. I would pray for wisdom, direction, and the strength to keep moving forward, even when the path wasn't clear.

As I stepped into my calling, I realized that it wasn't going to look like what I thought. The more I prayed, the more God revealed that my journey wasn't just about building a successful business— it was about building people. Nerdermar Catering became more than a service; it was a platform for God's work. Each event, each meal prepared, and each person served became an opportunity to show God's love, kindness, and entertain His presence. But stepping into my calling wasn't without challenges. There were times when I felt overwhelmed, especially when the business slowed down, or when things didn't go as planned. I had to constantly remind myself that God was in control, and that I was moving according to His timeline, not mine. I remember one time, after a particularly difficult week, I sat in prayer asking God, "Is this really what you want me to do?" And the answer was clear. He told me that success in His eyes wasn't measured the way the world measures it. It wasn't about how many events I catered or how much money I made. It was about how obedient I was to His voice, and how much I allowed Him to use me to serve others.

During this time, Bryan played a significant role in encouraging me. He was my constant reminder of what it looked like to love unconditionally and support someone without asking for anything in return. His presence helped me understand that God was teaching me to be both a servant and a leader. And that leadership didn't always come from a position of power or control, but from a place of humility, where you're willing to serve others even when you feel like you have nothing left to give. I had moments where I felt like I wasn't doing enough, or that I wasn't good enough to fulfill the vision God had given me. That's when God would remind me of the story of Moses. Moses didn't feel qualified either. He questioned God when he was called to lead the Israelites out of Egypt. But God wasn't looking for someone perfect—He was looking for someone willing. And that's what I had to be. Willing to serve. Willing to be used. Willing to step out in faith, even when I didn't see the whole picture.

It wasn't long before I started seeing the fruits of my obedience. The more I submitted to God's plan, the more doors began to open. Opportunities that I hadn't even imagined started to come my way. People were drawn to the way I did business, but it wasn't just the food—it was the love and care behind it. And that's when I realized, this was part of my ministry: feeding people, nurturing them, and creating an atmosphere of peace and love. That was God working through me, and with every new level came new challenges. There were days when I questioned if I was enough, if I was capable of doing what God had called me to do. But in those moments, I leaned into the lessons He had already taught me. I had to remind myself that God had been with me through the hardest parts of my journey, and He wasn't going to leave me now.

Chapter 20
Freed from Identity Prison

"He broke the box- I found my name."

O ne of the most powerful revelations I had during this journey was about identity. For a long time, I thought my identity was tied to what I did—my work, my business, my success. Yet God showed me that my identity wasn't in what I did, but in who I was in Him. This was a hard lesson to learn, because like many people, I had spent most of my life trying to prove myself—trying to show the world that I was worth something by what I could achieve. It became clear to me when I had a season where nothing seemed to be working. The business wasn't taking off the way I wanted, I felt overwhelmed with personal struggles, and I started questioning everything. I remember crying out to God, asking Him why He wasn't blessing my efforts. And that's when He revealed something profound to me: I was working out of a place of striving instead of surrender. I was trying to earn His love and approval, instead of resting in the fact that I already had it.

God took me to the story of Mary and Martha in Luke Chapter 10: Martha was busy, stressed, and worried about making sure everything was perfect, while Mary simply sat at the feet of Jesus. Martha, like me, was doing good things—she was serving. But Jesus told her that Mary had chosen the better part, to be in His presence and rest in Him. That hit me deeply. I realized that I had been living like Martha, constantly doing, constantly striving, and thinking that my worth came from how much I could accomplish. But what God was calling me to do was be more like Mary—sitting at His feet, finding peace in His presence, and understanding that my worth wasn't tied to what I could do, but to who I was in Him. This revelation shifted everything. It allowed me to release the pressure I was putting on myself to be perfect, to achieve more, and to constantly prove that I was enough. God showed me that I didn't need to hustle for His approval. He wasn't looking at my successes or failures—He was looking at my heart. And when I started to rest in that truth, I began to feel a freedom I had never felt before. I started making more time for quiet moments with God, letting Him pour into me, instead of always trying to pour out. I learned that my value wasn't based on what I could produce, but on the simple fact that I was His daughter, *and that was enough*. This truth transformed the way I approached both my personal life and my business. Instead of feeling like I had to carry the weight of everything on my shoulders, I learned to trust God more, knowing that He was the one in control.

Chapter 21
New Identity In Christ

"I don't fit the old version of me."

As I started to embrace this new understanding of identity, it brought a deep sense of relief, but it also challenged me in unexpected ways. When God strips you of the belief that your worth is tied to your performance, He also starts to highlight areas where you've been allowing that mindset to drive your relationships.

One of the biggest shifts was in how I related to people, especially Bryan. For a long time, I approached relationships from a place of wanting to earn love, approval, and acceptance. I thought if I could be the "perfect" partner or friend, then I would deserve love. But here's the thing—true love isn't something you can earn. It's a gift, and you have to be willing to receive it. This revelation became really clear in my relationship with Bryan. When we started courting, I constantly felt like I had to "prove" that I was worthy of the kind of love he was offering. I was used to dysfunctional relationships where I had to bend over backward just to feel valued. But Bryan's love was different—it was steady, patient, and didn't come with strings attached. And that scared me. I realized that my past experiences had trained me to believe that love was something you had to fight for or suffer for. But God was using Bryan to show me a different kind of love—a love that wasn't based on my performance or how much I gave. It was simply there, available, and unconditional.

This led to another important revelation: the love God has for me isn't based on how well I perform, but on who He created me to be. Just like Bryan's love wasn't conditional, neither was God's. But that also meant I had to stop putting up walls and running when I felt vulnerable or unworthy. There was a specific moment when this hit me. I remember feeling overwhelmed one night because Bryan had done something so simple yet so thoughtful— it was just one of those "I'm thinking of you" moments. Instead of feeling loved, I immediately felt guilty, like I didn't deserve it. I told myself, "He doesn't know the real me. If he knew all my flaws, all the things I've done, he wouldn't be this kind to me." But God stopped me right there. He whispered, "You don't have to be perfect to be loved. You just have to be willing to receive it. That's when I understood something profound: I had been rejecting love, not because it wasn't offered, but because I didn't believe I deserved it. The truth is, none of us can ever fully deserve love— especially the kind of love God gives. It's not about deserving; it's about accepting. That moment of revelation opened my heart even more to Bryan, but more importantly, it opened my heart to God in a way that I had never experienced before. I learned to let go of the fear that I wasn't enough, because in God's eyes, I am enough simply because He says so. It's a love that doesn't depend on what I do, but on who He is. That's the love I'm learning to walk in, and it's a love that is transforming not only how I see myself but how I relate to others.

Have you ever found yourself pushing away love because you felt undeserving? That's a question I asked myself over and over during this journey. If you've been there, this part of the process is about learning to accept love—God's love, and the love from others around you—without condition. As I began to understand that love isn't earned, but freely given, it became clear that trusting God required the same openness. If I couldn't accept love from Bryan without questioning it, how could I fully trust God's love without putting up my own conditions or walls?

The deeper dive into trust began with a question: What am I afraid of losing if I truly open myself to God's love and the love of others? I realized that the fear wasn't just about losing control or getting hurt—it was about losing the image of strength I had built for myself over the years. I had always been the one who could handle things, the one who didn't need anyone, the one who was independent and self-sufficient. But what God was showing me was that, in truth, I was afraid of vulnerability. I was afraid that if I let people in, they would see the broken parts of me that I had worked so hard to hide. I thought that being strong meant keeping those parts hidden. But God's love isn't about hiding—it's about healing.

Trusting God required me to drop my guard, to stop hiding behind the masks of independence and strength. I had to let Him see all of me, including the parts I didn't want to acknowledge—the fears, the insecurities, the pain from past relationships, and even the doubts I had about whether I was truly lovable. I remember being in prayer one night, asking God why it was so hard for me to fully trust Him. I had seen His hand in my life; I knew He had brought me through so many things. Yet there was still this hesitation, this part of me that held back. And in the quiet, He revealed something to me: "You think trust is about not getting hurt, but it's about knowing that even if you do, I will heal you." That was the breakthrough moment. I realized that trust wasn't about avoiding pain or hardship; it was about believing that God would be with me through it all and that His love would sustain me, no matter what. I had been so focused on protecting myself that I missed the essence of trust—it's not about avoiding the fall, it's about knowing that God will catch you, even when you stumble.

This revelation started to change how I approached my relationship with Bryan as well. For the first time, I could see that my walls weren't protecting me—they were keeping me from experiencing the fullness of love. I had to stop expecting everything to be perfect before I let myself be vulnerable. I had to trust that God had placed Bryan in my life for a reason and that part of that reason was to teach me how to receive love, not just give it. One specific moment stands out. Bryan had been trying to talk to me about something simple—something about our plans for the weekend—but I felt myself pulling back, feeling defensive for no reason. It was like my mind went into protection mode, assuming that I needed to guard myself. I paused, and in that moment, God whispered, "Trust. Let go. Just trust." I looked at Bryan and realized he wasn't trying to challenge me or criticize me—he was trying to connect. And my fear of being hurt or not being enough was causing me to distance myself from someone who genuinely loved me. In that moment, I chose to let my guard down, to let love in without questioning it. It was a small step, but it felt monumental.

The more I practiced trusting Bryan, the more I realized that this was God teaching me how to trust Him. Because in reality, the two were connected. How could I say I trusted God fully if I didn't trust the people He placed in my life to love me? That's when I really began to see that trust is built through surrender—through allowing God to take control, even when it feels risky. And here's the thing: the more I surrendered, the more peace I found. The more I let go of trying to protect myself, the more I saw how deeply God had already protected me, even from things I wasn't aware of. It was like a new layer of my relationship with God was being uncovered. I began to understand that trust was less about knowing all the answers or having everything figured out, and more about walking in faith, even when I didn't see the full picture. And that's the beauty of trust—it's a journey, not a destination. You don't arrive at trust; you build it over time, with each step of faith, each moment of vulnerability. I realized that trusting God means believing that He loves me enough to carry me through whatever comes my way. It means believing that His plans for me are good, even when they don't make sense at the moment. It means being okay with the fact that I won't always know what's next, but I can still walk forward, trusting that He's already gone ahead of me. This is the kind of trust that I'm learning to walk in daily—the trust that allows me to open my heart fully to God's love and the love of those He's placed in my life. It's a trust that says, "Even when it's hard, even when I don't understand, I know You've got me, God."

Chapter 22
Jesus, The Architect

"Every piece has purpose in His hands."

As I continued to walk in this newfound trust, I began to notice how it impacted not only my relationship with God and Bryan but also the way I viewed my purpose and future. Trusting God, in its truest sense, meant that I could no longer rely on my old ways of planning or achieving things in my own strength. I had to fully surrender even my goals and dreams to Him. Before this journey, I had a specific vision for my life. I thought I knew exactly what I wanted and how I was going to get there. But as I allowed God to reshape my heart, He also began to reshape my plans. It wasn't that I had to give up on my dreams, but rather that I needed to let go of my idea of how they should unfold. Trusting God meant believing that His way would be better—even if it looked different from what I had originally envisioned.

I started to ask myself hard questions: What if God's plan for me was bigger than I had imagined? What if the things I had been working so hard to achieve were only a small part of the bigger picture He had in mind? One night, in my quiet time with God, I felt Him pressing me to release everything into His hands—my catering business, my relationship with Bryan, even the dreams I had for my family and future. He asked me, "Are you willing to let go of your plans so I can give you My best?" It was a moment of deep surrender. Up until that point, I had been holding onto control in so many areas, thinking that if I could just work hard enough or plan well enough, everything would fall into place. But God was showing me that His blessings weren't something I could force or manipulate. They would come as I trusted and followed His lead. I remember praying that night, "Lord, I give it all to You. I release my timeline, my expectations, and my fears. I trust that Your plans are better than mine. Your word said in Ephesians 3:20, 'Now unto him that is able to do exceeding abundantly above all that we ask or think, according to the power that worketh in us.' Even if they look different from what I've been working toward, I trust that they will bring me closer to You." From that moment on, something shifted inside of me. I started to approach everything differently—whether it was making decisions for my business, planning my future with Bryan, or even just my daily routines. I began to operate from a place of faith instead of fear. I no longer felt the need to have everything figured out because I knew that God was in control.

My focus shifted from achieving to being—being available for whatever God wanted to do in and through me. This new posture of trust also helped me embrace the idea that my purpose wasn't just about what I did—it was about who I was becoming in

Christ. For so long, I had measured my success by external achievements, but now I understood that true success was about allowing God to shape my character, to make me more like Him. As I leaned into this, doors began to open in ways I hadn't expected. Opportunities came my way that I hadn't even been searching for—whether it was new clients for the catering business or new ways to serve in my community. It was like God was showing me that when I put Him first and trusted His timing, He would take care of everything else. And Bryan, who had been by my side through all of this, became a constant reminder of God's faithfulness. Our relationship was not just about companionship—it was about purpose. I could see how God had aligned us, not just for the sake of being together, but to fulfill a greater purpose in His kingdom. I began to realize that our partnership was part of God's plan to refine and prepare us for the next season of life. Looking back, I can see how every obstacle, every heartbreak, and every moment of uncertainty was leading me to this deeper revelation of trust. Each step of the journey was necessary to bring me to a place where I could finally release control and let God take the lead.

Let me be clear, trust is not a one-time decision—it's a daily choice. There are still days when fear or doubt creeps in, but now I have the tools to overcome them. I remind myself of God's promises, I look back at how far He's brought me, and I choose to believe that He will continue to guide me, even when I can't see the full picture. This is the season I'm in now—a season of trusting God with my whole heart, even when the path ahead is uncertain. And as I continue to trust Him, I know that He will continue to reveal His plans for my life, step by step. I encourage anyone reading this to take that same step of faith. Whatever you're holding onto, whatever you're afraid to let go of—surrender it to God. Trust that He has something greater in store for you, something that goes beyond what you could ever imagine. And know that as you walk in trust, He will never leave you or forsake you. His plans are good, and His timing is perfect.

Chapter 23
Ministry Unlocked

"What God placed in me can't stay locked."

Trusting God not only began to reshape my personal life, but it also profoundly transformed the way I approached my business, Nerdermar Catering. Before, I viewed the catering business as simply a means to an end—a way to support myself and provide for my family. I loved what I did, but I didn't fully grasp how much God could use this business as a ministry. I had placed limits on it, confining it to my own understanding. Yet, as I surrendered more and more to God, I started to realize that Nerdermar Catering wasn't just a business—it was a platform for ministry. God began to show me that He could use every interaction, every meal, and every event to touch lives. It was no longer just about providing food; it was about being a vessel for His love, His peace, and His presence to reach people in unexpected ways.

One of the first signs of this shift was how I began to pray over every event. I remember this one time when I was catering for a women's conference. In the past, I would've focused solely on the logistics—making sure the food was perfect, the presentation flawless, and the clients happy. But this time, I felt led to pray before I even started preparing the food. I asked God to not only bless the meal but also to allow His Spirit to flow through that event. I prayed that whoever ate the food would experience God's peace and joy, that it would nourish them beyond the physical. It wasn't just that people enjoyed the food—there was something deeper happening. I could feel the presence of God in that room, as if the atmosphere had changed. Conversations that started off light turned into deeper discussions about faith and healing. One woman approached me afterward, thanking me for the food, then she said something that left me speechless. She said, "I don't know what it was, but there was something about this meal, I can say God has truly blessed your hands". That moment was a confirmation for me. God was using Nerdermar Catering to do more than just fill bellies—He was using it to touch hearts and heal wounds. And that's when I knew that every meal I prepared, every event I catered, could be an opportunity for God to work in someone's life.

This shift in perspective changed everything. I began to approach each event with a sense of purpose and expectation. It wasn't just about the food anymore; it was about being a conduit for God's love. Whether I was serving at a conference, a retreat, or a family gathering, I started to pray over each dish, asking God to use it as a tool for His glory.

One of the most powerful moments came during a marriage retreat I catered. I had already shared how God had opened the door for me to be the chef for that event, and I knew He had a purpose for me being there beyond just cooking. I remember standing in the kitchen, praying over the meals as I prepared them. I asked God to bless the couples who would be eating, to bring healing to their marriages, and to restore whatever was broken. Throughout that weekend, I could see the way God was moving. Couples who had been distant started to open up to each other. There were moments of deep forgiveness and reconciliation, and I knew that God was doing something powerful in that space.

As I continued to step into this new understanding, I noticed that more opportunities began to open up. People started to reach out to me not just because of my food but because they sensed something different about Nerdermar Catering. They could feel that there was something deeper happening, that it wasn't just about business—it was about ministry. This was when I started to think of my business not just as a catering service, but as a "traveling table of grace." Whether I was cooking for a large event or preparing a private meal for a family, I approached each moment with the mindset that this was God's table, and everyone who sat at it would experience His love and grace.

It wasn't always easy, though. There were times when I was tempted to fall back into old habits, to focus more on the business side of things and less on the ministry aspect. But each time, God gently reminded me that this was His business, and if I trusted Him, He would take care of every need. And let me tell you, He has been faithful. There have been seasons when business was slow, and I wasn't sure how I would make ends meet. But God always provided. He would send the right clients at the right time, or He would open doors I hadn't even considered. I learned that when I placed the business in His hands, He took care of everything—even the details I hadn't thought of.

This journey has taught me that when you partner with God, there is no limit to what He can do. He will take the ordinary and make it extraordinary. He will use the things you never thought were significant and turn them into tools for His kingdom. Nerdermar Catering has become more than I ever imagined, not because of anything I've done, but because I've allowed God to lead the way. Now, I approach each day with a sense of excitement and anticipation, knowing that God can use even the smallest act of service to make a big impact. Whether I'm cooking for one person or a hundred, I know that God is at work, and that makes all the difference.

Chapter 24
His Thoughts are not My Thoughts

"In His wisdom, every delay is divine direction."

Trusting God continued to reveal layers of His plan that I had not anticipated. As Nerdermar Catering grew, so did my understanding of how God was using my business as a ministry. What I didn't realize was that this journey of faith and surrender was about preparing me for a much larger purpose, one that would touch many areas of my life.

I clearly recall a season where I felt like God was pressing me even deeper into reliance on Him. Business was slower than usual, and I found myself wondering, "God, what now?" It's funny how we can walk in faith for a while and see God move, but then doubt creeps in again when things don't go according to our plans. That was where I found myself—wavering, unsure, and feeling the weight of my responsibilities. Yet in that season, God didn't just provide materially, He took me to another level spiritually. He was teaching me that my trust couldn't be dependent on whether things were going well or not. It had to be a steady, unwavering trust, even when the outcome wasn't clear. This was a hard lesson, but it was one that shifted everything for me. I'll never forget the moment when, in the middle of that uncertainty, a friend called me out of the blue to ask if I could cater for an event. It wasn't a large event by any means—just a small family gathering—but it was a divine appointment. During that event, I felt led to share my story with one of the guests. I didn't know why, but I trusted that God had brought me there for more than just the food. As I shared about my journey of healing and forgiveness, I could discern the walls breaking down in this person's heart. We ended up praying together, and she later told me that conversation was exactly what she needed at that moment.

It was then that I realized God's purpose for me was expanding. Nerdermar Catering wasn't just about providing a physical service—it was about creating moments where people could encounter God. I understood that every single event, no matter how small, was an opportunity for ministry. This shift in perspective was key. It wasn't just about seeing the business as a ministry anymore—it was about seeing my entire life as a platform for God to move. Every conversation, every interaction, every moment became a potential divine appointment. And I started to live with that expectation, knowing that God could use the simplest things to do the most profound work. Let me tell you, living with that level of openness wasn't easy. There were times when I wanted to retreat, to go back to the comfortable, to not have to be "on mission" all the time. It can be exhausting when you feel like you're constantly being stretched. But God reminded me time and time again that His grace was sufficient, that He would supply the strength and the wisdom when I needed it.

It was during one of those stretching seasons that God began to reveal something else to me—something deeply personal. I had come so far in my healing journey, but there were still areas of my life that I hadn't fully surrendered. One of those areas was my sense of identity and worth. As much as I had grown, there were still moments when I struggled with self-doubt, with feeling like I wasn't enough. This was especially true when it came to relationships. As Bryan continued to court me, I realized that God was using this relationship to reveal parts of myself that I hadn't fully dealt with. Bryan, being the kind and patient man he is, never rushed me through the process. He allowed me to feel what I needed to feel, and he was always there to support me. But it was God who was doing the deeper work in my heart, showing me that my identity wasn't in what I did or how I performed—it was in who He said I was.

One of the most powerful moments in that season was when I finally admitted to God that I had been hiding behind my independence. For so long, I prided myself on being able to do things on my own, on not needing anyone. But the truth was, I had been using that independence as a shield to protect myself from being vulnerable, from being hurt. And God was gently showing me that in order to experience the fullness of His love, I needed to let go of that shield. This wasn't an overnight process. It took time—prayer, reflection, and a lot of hard conversations with God and with myself. But slowly, I began to let go. I began to see that true strength wasn't about being self-reliant, but about being reliant on God. True strength was about being willing to be vulnerable, to admit when I needed help, and to trust that God would provide the support I needed. Bryan was a big part of that process. He was the one God used to show me what healthy love looked like, and it was through his patience and care that I began to understand more fully what it meant to be loved without conditions. There were many times when I would push him away, not because I didn't care for him, but because I was afraid of being hurt again. Yet each time, he would remind me that he wasn't going anywhere, that he was committed to walking this journey with me.

Through all of this, God was refining me. He was stripping away the lies I had believed about myself, about love, and about what it meant to be whole. He was showing me that I didn't have to have it all together, that it was okay to have weaknesses, and that His strength was made perfect in those weaknesses. It's amazing how God works. In the areas where I felt the most broken, He was bringing the most healing. In the spaces where I felt the most unqualified, He was equipping me for His purpose. And through it all, He was reminding me that this journey wasn't just about me—it was about Him. It was about His glory, His grace, and His ability to take the most unlikely person and use them for something extraordinary.

Chapter 25
Learning Balance

"It's not about doing it all- it's about doing it with Him."

Navigating my relationship with my children while living apart was a journey in itself. They were in Jamaica with my mother, and despite the distance, we maintained a close bond through WhatsApp and regular prayers together. This connection was crucial, especially when challenges arose. When my children faced difficulties, including the incident where my eldest was injured, it was a wake-up call for me. It highlighted the high expectations I had placed on my mother and the impact of those expectations on our family dynamics. I realized that in order to heal and move forward, I needed to release these expectations and forgive both my mother and myself.

The process of forgiveness was intense and required me to revisit old wounds and childhood traumas. By addressing these issues, I learned to set healthy boundaries and embrace the *ministry of reconciliation* as outlined in 2 Corinthians 5. This meant forgiving my mother and reestablishing our relationship with clear, loving boundaries. Forgiveness was not just for my mother but also for my own healing. It allowed me to move past the resentment and anger that had been clouding my judgment. As a result, I was better equipped to support my children and be present in their lives despite the physical distance. Over time, I've seen growth in myself and in how I interact with my children. This journey of forgiveness and healing has given me a clearer perspective on my role as a parent and has improved our relationship. By continuously working on my own emotional health, I've been able to offer better support and guidance to my children, even from afar.

The decision to change my children's school was a necessary step in their growth and well-being. It wasn't just about finding a better educational environment; it was also about creating stability and addressing the challenges they were facing. Transitioning to a new school meant new routines, new teachers, and new classmates. For my children, it was an adjustment period filled with mixed emotions. They had to adapt to a new learning environment while processing the changes happening in our family dynamics. Throughout this transition, I maintained open lines of communication with them. We continued our regular WhatsApp calls and prayers, which helped them feel supported despite the upheaval. I made sure to stay engaged in their academic and social lives, showing them that I was there for them, no matter the distance. The change in school also provided an opportunity for me to reflect on my role as a parent and how I could better support my children through these transitions. It reinforced the importance of resilience and adaptability, for them and for me.

This period of adjustment wasn't without its challenges, but it also brought growth and new perspectives. As my children began to settle into their new school, I saw them gradually adjusting and thriving in their new environment. This experience was a reminder of the strength and flexibility within our family and the power of staying connected and supportive through life's changes.

Now that my children are living with their dad, I'm aware that this new environment presents its own set of challenges. He is navigating his own childhood trauma and healing process, which affects the household dynamics. It's not the ideal environment I had hoped for, but with God's presence in the midst of this storm, we find strength and hope. Even though the situation isn't perfect, I continue to pray for healing and restoration, for my children and their dad. I trust that God is working in their lives, even when the path seems uncertain. Staying connected with my children through regular communication and prayers helps me maintain a sense of peace. I encourage them to lean on their faith and trust that God is guiding them through this time. By focusing on the positives and maintaining hope, I can smile through the storm, knowing that God's grace and love are ever-present. This chapter in our lives may be challenging, but it also offers opportunities for growth and deeper faith. I remain committed to supporting my children and trusting that, with God's help, they will navigate these challenges and emerge stronger.

In this challenging season, I've found solace in the words of Jeremiah 29:11, which has become a cornerstone of my faith. The verse says, "For I know the plans I have for you, declares the Lord, plans to prosper you and not to harm you, plans to give you hope and a future" (NIV). Whenever I face difficulties with my children or the situation seems overwhelming, this promise reminds me that God has a purpose and a plan for us, even when the path isn't clear. This verse provides me with comfort and strength, assuring me that despite the current hardships, God's plans are filled with hope and prosperity for my family. It's a source of encouragement and a reminder that God's guidance is always present, leading us through every storm and challenge. By holding onto this promise, I am able to remain hopeful and focused on the positive outcomes that God has in store for us. It helps me navigate the difficulties with faith and trust, knowing that God's plan is always for our good.

Chapter 26
Leaving no Stones Unturned

"What wounded them won't rule me."

Here I am, reflecting on the journey of forgiveness. I initially thought my mother was the one who needed forgiveness, but God revealed a deeper layer. He guided me through a second phase of forgiveness, where I had to turn to both parents, my mom and my dad. I needed to ask them for forgiveness for the unrealistic expectations I had placed on them. This revelation helped me see that forgiveness was not just about healing the past hurts but also about releasing the burden of expectations that I had imposed. It was a powerful step in reconciling my relationships and finding peace within myself. So, in this journey, I learned that forgiveness is not just about letting go of past hurts. It's also about recognizing and releasing the expectations I had imposed on my parents. By asking them for forgiveness, I was able to clear out the emotional baggage and find a deeper sense of peace and healing. It transformed not just my relationships with them but also how I see and handle my own life; growth is an ongoing process. Even as you work through your challenges and learn from them, it's important to remember that you're still evolving and being shaped. Each step, whether it's a breakthrough or a struggle, contributes to the person you're becoming. I also learned something profound when God asked me, "What about you?" I never thought about forgiving myself until the Lord revealed it.

We often limit our view of what God can do based on our own understanding and experiences. But God operates beyond our expectations and can bring about results far greater than we can imagine. His ways and thoughts are so much higher than ours. In our humanness, we might try to confine God to our own plans and dreams. Yet, His plans are infinitely better and more expansive. Trusting in His higher wisdom means letting go of our own constraints and allowing Him to guide us toward blessings and breakthroughs that we couldn't have envisioned on our own. It's a journey of faith, where we surrender our limited vision for His boundless possibilities. "For my thoughts *are* not your thoughts, neither *are* your ways my ways," declares the Lord. "As the heavens are higher than the earth, so are my ways higher than your ways and my thoughts than your thoughts" (Isaiah 55:8-9 NIV). Embracing this truth requires us to let go of control and trust that God's timing and plans are perfect, even when they seem uncertain or challenging. As we navigate our personal struggles and growth, recognizing that God's understanding far surpasses our own helps us remain steadfast and hopeful. It's about learning to walk in faith, knowing that every step, no matter how difficult, is leading us toward His greater purpose and grace.

Chapter 27
Embracing Growth

"God never wastes growth; He uses it to reveal His glory."

As I reflect on my journey, I realize that God has always been orchestrating everything for my growth and His glory. Even when I didn't understand the pain, the delays, or the challenges, I now see that they were necessary for shaping me into who I am today. His ways truly aren't our ways. Where I expected answers to come in a particular form, God's plan was far beyond my limited understanding. Each trial I've faced has brought me closer to Him, allowing me to release my past, forgive, and move forward with a new understanding of grace. My relationship with God has deepened as I've come to trust Him more with every aspect of my life—my children, my relationships, my work, and my calling. Along with healing me, God revealed He also wanted to refine me and turn my scars into testimonies. I'm learning that every wound has the potential to bear fruit if surrendered to Him. It's in these moments of surrender where transformation happens, and now, I look at challenges differently, knowing that God can use them to build something new in me.

I remembered my spiritual mother telling me that God wouldn't take five years to use me for His glory. She said it would be different. A few months after that, I was graced by God to start my ministry, called "Mountain Overcomers." In that same season I hosted my first women's conference. You can't imagine how many times I went back to God, asking if He was sure I was the person for the job. During the preparation for the conference, I had my Moses moment: "God, I'm not eloquent enough." I felt like Isaiah saying, "Here I am, send me," but also like Elisha in 2 Kings, who was determined to follow Elijah no matter how the other prophets tried to distract him. Elisha was adamant about continuing until the end, and that was me throughout the planning process. I didn't understand everything, but I trusted God. My community fully supported me every step of the way. Every minute detail the Lord gave me—from the color scheme to the settings—was followed, and the outcome was fantastic. The conference took place in my birth month, and it felt like a divine gift. People were poured into, and they left feeling rejuvenated and renewed. Now, I have a monthly Zoom line to continue the healing process.

Let me say this, some Christians out there might make you feel like following Christ is a walk in the park. Now if you're reading this, you might be thinking, "One minute she's on top of the mountain, and the next she's in the valley." The truth is, the Bible tells us that Jesus said, "Take up your cross and follow me." You will experience highs and lows, but guess what? God is always with us, through every peak and valley. Am I perfect in my walk? No, I'm not, but I don't stay down. The Bible says, "For all have sinned, and come short of the glory of God" (Romans 3:23). We sin daily, and that's why there is repentance. It's a journey of growth, falling and getting back up, knowing that God's grace is always there to restore us.

The Christian Walk as a Mountain Climb and Butterfly

In my journey with God, I've come to see that the Christian walk is like climbing a mountain. Every part of the mountain represents a stage of growth, challenge, or reflection: the base of the mountain is where I started. The base represents the beginning of my faith journey, accepting Christ. It's easy to look up and see how far I have to go, but at this point, I was full of excitement, unaware of the battles ahead. The Base is where the foundation is laid, and the climb begins. The Steep Climb–the next stage is the steep climb. Here, the path isn't easy. It's where I encountered trials— unforgiveness, childhood trauma, and learning to forgive my parents. The air gets thinner, and each step requires more effort. Just like in life, God doesn't always remove the obstacles; He uses them to make me stronger. Every step of the steep climb was a test of endurance and faith, just like it was for Elisha following Elijah, determined not to stop halfway. The Rocky Paths–sometimes, the path becomes rocky and uncertain. I would stumble, fall, and get hurt. There were times when I wanted to give up, questioning if I was fit for the calling. Like when I doubted whether I was the one to host the Mountain Overcomers Ministry. But these rocks were also moments of learning, times when God refined me, as Job said, to come forth as gold. The Summit–reaching the summit isn't about perfection but perseverance. At moments of victory,

when I hosted the Women's Ministry conference or led a successful Zoom session, I felt as though I had reached the top, basking
in God's glory. But every summit prepares me for the next climb,
just as every season of growth leads to deeper faith and more responsibility. Transformation of a Butterfly: Just as the climb up
the mountain shapes my faith, so too does the process of
transformation resemble that of a butterfly. At the start of my
journey, I was a caterpillar, crawling and bound by earthly limita-
tions. The struggles I faced—the pain, unforgiveness, self-
doubt—were the cocoon around me. The caterpillar doesn't understand the transformation happening in the cocoon, just as I
didn't fully understand what God was doing in my life. But once
I surrendered to His process, once I allowed Him to work in me
through trials, I emerged transformed—just like a butterfly. Free
to soar, released from the bondage of past hurts, ready to embrace
the beauty of God's purpose in my life.

Biblical Mountain Experiences: Encounters with God

In the Bible, many of God's most powerful revelations took place
on mountains, symbolizing a higher plane of understanding and
intimacy with Him. These moments of divine encounter didn't
just change individual lives but often marked pivotal shifts for
entire nations or faith journeys. Let's explore some of the most
notable figures who met God on the mountaintop:

Moses: Mount Sinai (Exodus 19-20, 24)

Moses' encounter with God on Mount Sinai is one of the most
well-known mountain experiences in the Bible. Here, God gave

Moses the Ten Commandments and revealed His covenant with Israel. Moses' time on the mountain wasn't just a personal encounter—it was a moment of national transformation. God's glory descended like a consuming fire, and through Moses, He established the law that would guide His people. This meeting is symbolic of divine order, revelation, and guidance.

Elijah: Mount Carmel (1 Kings 18)

Elijah's showdown with the prophets of Baal on Mount Carmel demonstrated the power of unwavering faith in God. Surrounded by opposition and disbelief, Elijah stood alone in faith and called upon God, who answered by fire. This encounter was a mountain experience of triumph and vindication, where God showed His supremacy over false gods. It was also a turning point for Israel, calling them back to worship the one true God.

Abraham: Mount Moriah (Genesis 22)

Abraham's journey to Mount Moriah is one of the most profound stories of faith and obedience in the Bible. God tested Abraham by asking him to sacrifice his son, Isaac. This mountain experience was one of ultimate surrender and trust in God. In the end, God provided a ram in place of Isaac, showing that obedience brings provision. Abraham encountered God as Jehovah Jireh, the Lord who provides.

Jesus: The Mount of Transfiguration (Matthew 17, Mark 9, Luke 9)

On this mountain, Jesus was transfigured before His disciples—His face shone like the sun, and His clothes became as white as light. Moses and Elijah appeared with Him, representing the law and the prophets. This mountain encounter confirmed Jesus' divinity and His fulfillment of God's promises. It was a moment of glory and revelation for Peter, James, and John, where they witnessed the true nature of Christ.

Noah: Mount Ararat (Genesis 8)

After the great flood, Noah's ark rested on Mount Ararat. This marked a new beginning for humanity, as God made a covenant with Noah, promising never to destroy the earth by flood again. The mountain experience of Noah represents restoration and a fresh start, with God's promise symbolized in the rainbow.

Jesus: Mount of Olives (Luke 22, Matthew 24)

Jesus spent significant time on the Mount of Olives, including during His final days before the crucifixion. It was here that He prayed in the Garden of Gethsemane, wrestling with the weight of what was to come. The Mount of Olives is a place of surrender, prayer, and preparation for the greatest act of love—Jesus' sacrifice on the cross.

Each of these mountain encounters shows us that meeting God often involves moments of revelation, sacrifice, obedience, and sometimes great trials. Just like the physical climb up a mountain, the spiritual climb brings us closer to God, pushing us to new heights in our faith. These biblical mountain experiences remind us that God meets us where we are and brings us to new levels of understanding and breakthrough.

My Mountaintop Experience:

Writing this book just as many of the great figures in the Bible encountered God on the mountaintop, I too had my own mountain experience. Writing this book was a journey that felt like climbing a steep mountain—filled with challenges, revelations, and moments of divine encounter. There were times when I doubted my ability to bring this project to life. Just like Moses questioned his eloquence, I wondered if I had the right words. I had my Elijah moments, standing against the overwhelming pressure to give up, and my Abraham moments of surrender, laying my own plans down and trusting that God had a purpose for this book. I felt the weight of responsibility to faithfully share my testimony, but just as God provided for each of these biblical figures, He provided for me. Each chapter, each revelation, felt like reaching a new height, bringing me closer to God's plan and purpose. There were moments of deep reflection, where I wrestled with my own struggles, my own valleys. But just like David, I pressed on, trusting that God was leading me through. The words flowed, sometimes effortlessly, and other times through great effort. But in the end, I knew that every word was ordained by Him. The top of this mountain was not just the completion of a book, but the beginning of a new chapter in my spiritual journey. I was able to look back at the climb—the valleys

I had passed through, the storms I had endured—and see how God had been with me all along. Writing this book became a symbol of victory, a testament to God's faithfulness in my life. Just like David's cup ran over after his valley experience, I too experienced an overflow. The process was not easy, but it was necessary. And standing on top of this mountain, I can say that every step was worth it. God revealed Himself to me in new ways through the writing of this book, and now, as I stand on this mountaintop, I am ready to share that revelation with you.

A Deeper Look into David's Words

Verse 1: "The Lord is my Shepherd; I shall not want." Here, David assures us that with God as our Shepherd, all our needs are met. The Hebrew word for "Shepherd" is Ra'ah, meaning to lead or tend. When we trust God, we lack nothing.

Verse 2: "He maketh me to lie down in green pastures: He leadeth me beside the still waters." Imagine a cow grazing peacefully in a lush pasture; this is God's promise to provide and protect us. Just as the still waters reflect tranquility, we can find peace in Him.

Verse 3: "He restoreth my soul; He leadeth me in the paths of righteousness for His name's sake." David reminds us that God restores and guides us. When we follow His path, righteousness will always lead us to the right outcome.

Verse 4: "Yea, though I walk through the valley of the shadow of death, I will fear no evil; for Thou art with me." The key word here is "through." David shows us that while we may walk through dark valleys, we do not walk alone. God's presence brings comfort.

Verse 5: "Thou preparest a table before me in the presence of mine enemies: Thou anointest my head with oil; my cup runneth over." Here, God honors us in front of our adversaries. The overflow in our lives comes from God's blessings amidst our struggles.

Verse 6: "Surely goodness and mercy shall follow me all the days of my life, and I will dwell in the house of the Lord forever." David concludes with a declaration of faith. Knowing God's goodness and mercy follows us brings assurance and strength to face any mountain or valley.

Finding Comfort and Strength

Psalms 23 serves as a powerful reminder of God's faithfulness in every season of our lives. It encourages us to trust Him fully, whether on the mountain or in the valley.

Closing

Walking in Purpose

As I bring this book to a close, I want to remind you that this is only the beginning. Life will always present mountains and valleys, victories and challenges, but one thing remains true, God is with you through it all. He never leaves, and He never forsakes.

If there's one take away I hope you leave with, it's this: Trust the process. Your journey may not look like anyone else's, but it is divinely crafted for you. There may be times when you feel unqualified, unseen or overwhelmed. Push past the fear, self doubt,and distractions. God doesn't make mistakes when He calls us, and His timing is always perfect.

I am living proof of what God can do when you say "Yes" despite the doubts and fears. From leaving Jamaica in obedience to His call, to building a ministry, becoming a certified mental health first aider, writing this book, and overcoming countless hurdles, I've learned that the valley only prepares you for the mountaintop. And trust me there's always another mountain waiting, but now you know the God who conquers them all.

Thank you for walking this journey with me. May this book encourage you to step boldly into your purpose, knowing that the Author and Finisher of our faith has already paved the way.

Keep climbing, keep trusting, and keep overcoming.

God bless you,

Jodi

www.ingramcontent.com/pod-product-compliance
Lightning Source LLC
Chambersburg PA
CBHW051326120626

46547CB00015B/2412